FLOWERS of Volunteer Park Conservatory

BLOOMING · MONTH · BY · MONTH

Sara L. Chapman

Book Publishers Network
P. O. Box 2256
Bothell, WA 98041
425.483.3040
www.bookpublishersnetwork.com

Copyright 2011 by Sara L. Chapman

www.lovethatimage.com

Library of Congress Control Number: 2011905677

Chapman, Sara L.

Flowers of Volunteer Park Conservatory Blooming Month By Month/
Sara L. Chapman
    Includes Index.

ISBN 10 1-935359-81-9 (hard cover)
ISBN 13 978-1-935359-81-4 (hard cover)

ISBN 10 1-935359-80-0 (soft cover)
ISBN 13 978-1-935359-80-7 (soft cover)

Printed in U.S.A. Last number indicates this printing.

10 9 8 7 6 5 4 3 2 1

Grateful acknowledgement to those who helped with the huge job of horticultural plant identification. Thank you to Sara Lawrence, Volunteer for FOC and Conservatory Greenhouse; Giselle Blythe, Conservatory Gardener; David Helgeson, Conservatory Senior Gardener; Jeanne Schollmeyer, Conservatory Gardener; Johan Schorer, Jefferson Greenhouse Senior Gardener; Nancy Cifuentes, Volunteer Park Gardener; and Michael Cory, Conservatory Volunteer in orchid collection and docent.

Author photograph: Alyssa Rose Photography

Introduction

Welcome to Seattle's hidden gem, the historic Volunteer Park Conservatory. Enjoy a photographic tour of its extraordinary flower and foliage collections and their changes, month by month, throughout the year. If you are lucky enough to have visited the Conservatory this may be a stroll down memory lane for you. Look for the flower favorites you remember, or find new plant thrills. This book can help plan future visits, or inspire you to try growing new plants in your own home or garden. But in any case, the beauty of the world-class Conservatory's flowers and the fascination of its plants are in your hands.

Explore the five Houses (see Floor Plan on page 135: the Palm House with its incredible orchid collection; the Seasonal House with its ever-changing show of spring, summer, fall and winter blooming bliss; the Cactus House with its intriguing cacti, succulents and flowers throughout the year; the Fern House with its tropical flowers, carnivorous plants and the meditative pool; and the Bromeliad House, home to pineapple plants, air plants and even more exotic flowers. Every single visit reveals something new and different in every nook of the Conservatory.

While not a complete catalogue of the Conservatory's riches, my hope is that this personal view, created from twelve visits—one each month—will delight and inform you. Please see the Keys to Plant Identification starting on page 128, created by Sara Lawrence and Giselle Blythe, to learn more about many of the plants you see in these pages. Test your knowledge!

The Conservatory displays do vary from week to week, month to month and from year to year, depending on many factors including the weather, plant development stage, availability, and the artistic inspiration of the Conservatory's gifted Senior Gardener, David Helgeson. Visit often!

Essential to the beauty of the displays is the effort of many volunteers. When you visit in person, do visit the Gift Shop, a plant-related jewel of a shop with its staff a source of very helpful information. Consider supporting the Conservatory by joining the Friends of the Conservatory, established in 1980, to help with its mission of advocacy, support of the plant collections, public participation and education.

— Sara L. Chapman
Seattle, Washington
July 2011

Foreword *by David Helgeson*

Since 1912 the Volunteer Park Conservatory has attracted visitors from near and far. Long hailed as the "Jewel in the Crown" of Seattle's park system, the Conservatory has been a source of local pride and a welcome sanctuary from the frenetic pace of urban life.

This graceful, Victorian-style structure is owned and operated by Seattle's Department of Parks and Recreation with strong support from the Friends of the Conservatory. The vision of the city's early civic leaders, our Conservatory is the focal point of the original Olmstead plan for the beautiful fifty-acre Volunteer Park situated at the north end of Seattle's vibrant Capitol Hill neighborhood.

A century of generous public donation and careful selection by horticulture staff has helped create one of the Pacific Northwest's premier tropical plant collections. Highlights include cacti and succulent species, bromeliads, epiphytes and terrestrial plants. Always a favorite attraction, the orchid collection, begun in 1921, has grown to one of the largest publicly held collections of its kind on the West coast. Arching palms, towering tree ferns and many unusual tropical plants with brilliant foliage patterns and colorful flowers provide a verdant and varied backdrop to the Conservatory experience.

The bulk of the permanent collections are held on site in the Conservatory's support greenhouses. Here the displays are started and grown, sometimes up to a year in advance. Plants for display are skillfully trained including applying the correct amount of light, fertilizer, pinching, pruning, and staking, prepared for display by senior gardener Jeanne Schollmeyer and her dedicated staff.

A frequent comment from visitors to the Conservatory is, "You must love your work!" Indeed, I consider it an honor and privilege to serve our guests in this enchanting environment. I invite you to visit and return often, to step back in time and enjoy a peaceful moment, or join us for one of our many educational offerings and participate first-hand in the future of this unique, historic site.

We hope to see you soon!

— David Helgeson
Senior Gardener
Volunteer Park Conservatory

Foreword *by Anthonio Pettit*

Every visit to Volunteer Park Conservatory is a unique experience. The magnificent collection housed within the proud glass framework is in itself a living organism, ever changing, growing and breathing. A first-time visitor might assume the displays remain static throughout the year, but in reality each of the houses are in a constant flurry of motion, rotating in the most extraordinary specimens as they come into bloom or bear unusual fruit. Less conspicuous is the complementary foliage tucked skillfully between the showpieces, creating a seamless wonderland year round. It's never the same twice!

However, while the Volunteer Park Conservatory has been a treasured, world-class destination in Seattle, serving countless thousands of visitors each year for the past century, it is crucial that we not take this jewel for granted. As we celebrate the Conservatory's 100th anniversary, let us not forget the commitment required by the City of Seattle to sustain such an exceptional resource.

Since 1980, the Friends of the Conservatory (FOC), the non-profit, community-based advocacy organization for the Volunteer Park Conservatory, has been dedicated to preservation, public participation and education. Through grassroots efforts and ongoing engagement, the FOC has been able to help keep the Conservatory's doors open to the public and the collections thriving.

We encourage everyone to witness the incredible variations throughout the year in person. With continued support from FOC members and the community, we will see the Conservatory remain vibrant through its second century and beyond!

— Anthonio Mighuel Bishop Pettit
President, Friends of the Conservatory

THE FRIENDS OF THE
CONSERVATORY

VOLUNTEER PARK

Behind the Scenes *by Sara Lawrence*

Upon first discovering the Volunteer Park Conservatory, many a visitor is struck with the realization that they've lucked into a world imagined, an ideal sort of place. This wonder naturally gives way to curiosity about what must go on behind the scenes to create such a fluid movement through five diverse bio-regions. If you could shine a light on the inner workings of the Conservatory, you would find a devoted team of gardeners and volunteers who research, grow, prepare for bloom, and continuously groom the plants in the four support greenhouses hidden just behind the crystal palace.

Six times each year this tight-knit team overhauls the Seasonal House. If you were to shadow our gardeners in January, you would learn that the azaleas, brought in from the winter cold, are encouraged to bloom with groups of cineraria and cyclamen. These are then replaced by hydrangeas and the hundreds of bulbs that were forced and made ready for display by February. Bleeding hearts are a brief addition in March, while the gardeners are busy preparing the chrysanthemums for autumn. By May the fuchsias have begun to open their huge and sensuous flowers like charmed earrings, and by mid-month there is a riot of coleus colors and smoky astilbe plumes, from shades of white to lavender. In June, hollyhocks and campanulas, started from seed nearly two years earlier, harmonize with the deep purple blue of delphiniums and kaleidoscope of salpiglossis. Soon the hot sizzle of cannas and oriental lilies kick in to create a cacophony of summer color into the autumn.

When September arrives, a quieter note begins. The chrysanthemums that were prepared in the spring will take the place of the summer perennials in the Seasonal House, soothing us with the honeyed tones of fall.

As daylight hours become precious, the Conservatory remains bright, warm, and welcoming. By December, the azaleas are being readied for spring once again, and we celebrate the quiet of winter with a display of multicolored poinsettias and a majestic noble fir tree festooned with mirrored ornaments and lights.

These pages reflect the Conservatory's magnificent collections that delight us daily. It also reflects the work of the volunteers who helped identify the plants for plant lovers of all levels. We are lucky to have a living landmark like the Conservatory to enjoy and share with each other. May it continue to be discovered and cherished, a garden no longer of the imagination.

— Sara Lawrence, Volunteer
Volunteer Park Conservatory

SEASONAL HOUSE

JANUARY

10

See page 128

SEASONAL HOUSE

Clockwise from upper left: White Cyclamen; West entry of Seasonal House; Stained glass window; Pink Azaleas

Bird of Paradise, *Strelitzia reginae*

PALM HOUSE

Spotted Lady Slipper Orchid, *Paphiopedilum* hybrid

Upper: Red Anthurium, *Anthurium andraeanum*
Lower: Scarlet Plume, *Euphorbia fulgens*

See page 128

FERN HOUSE

Lavender Bromeliad, *Guzmania* 'Grapeade'

BROMELIAD HOUSE

FEBRUARY

Red Bromeliad, *Guzmania* hybrid

Emerging Daffodils

OUTSIDE

Clockwise from upper left: Display with Azaleas, Maidenhair Ferns and Daffodils; Daffodils, *Narcissus* 'Ice Follies'; Florist Cyclamen, *Cyclamen persicum;* Pink Evergreen Florist Azalea, *Rhododendron* hybrid

Clockwise from upper left: *Agapetes serpens* (2 photos); Lemon Tree and Bromeliad display; Purple Bromeliad, *Neoregelia* hybrid.

BROMELIAD HOUSE

Lemon Tree, *Citrus limon*

Rieger Begonia, *Begonia x hiemalis;* Tiger Fern, *Nephrolepis exaltata* 'Tiger'

FERN HOUSE

Upper: Peacock Plant, *Calathea veitchiana*
Lower: *Aeschynanthus humilis*

See page 128

FEBRUARY

23

MARCH

Orchid, *Doritaenopsis* hybrid

PALM HOUSE

Orchids, clockwise from upper left: *Dendrobium* White Christmas 'Maiko'; *Doritaenopsis* Tai Lin Angel x *Doritaenopsis* hybrid; Yellow Lady Slipper, *Phragmipedium* Grande; *Oncidium* hybrid

MARCH

Clockwise from upper left: Easter Lily, *Lilium longiflorum* 'Nellie White'; Variegated Tulip buds; White Bleeding Heart, *Dicentra spectabilis alba;* Mophead Hydrangea, *Hydrangea macrophylla*

SEASONAL HOUSE

See page 128

See page 129

CACTUS HOUSE

Upper: Twin-spined Cactus, *Mammillaria geminispina*
Lower: Barrel Cactus, *Ferocactus glaucescens*

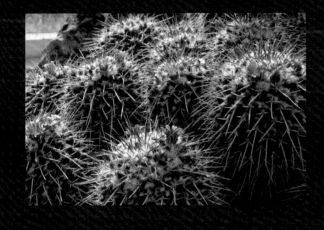

Texas Nipple Cactus, *Mammillaria prolifera*

MARCH

31

Lollipop Flower, *Pachystachys lutea*

Upper: Grape-leaf Passion Flower, *Passiflora vitifolia*
Lower: Blue Mist Flower, *Eupatorium atrorubens*

FERN HOUSE

See page 129

Pansies

APRIL

A

B

C

D

E

F

G

C

H

I

See page 129

Upper: Gardenia *jasminoides*
Lower: Fortnight Lily, *Dietes iridioide*

SEASONAL HOUSE

Blue Lacecap Hydrangea, *Hydrangea macrophylla* hybrid

Orchid Cactus, *Epicactus* hybrid

BROMELIAD & FERN HOUSES

Orchid Cactus, clockwise from upper left: Yellow, *Epicactus* 'Primary Ignition'; Coral Pink, *Epicactus* hybrid; Pink, *Epicactus* 'Sakurahime'; Magenta, *Epicactus* hybrid

Upper: Giant Spider Lily, *Crinum amabile*
Lower: Reiger Begonia, *Begonia x hiemalis*

Blue Sky Vine, *Thunbergia grandiflora*

FERN HOUSE

See page 129

CACTUS HOUSE

Upper: Desert Rose, *Adenium obesum*
Lower: Suzanne's Spurge, *Euphorbia suzannae*

Burro's Tail, *Sedum morganianum;* White Rhododendron outside

APRIL

Two Fuchsias and White Hydrangea

SEASONAL HOUSE

MAY

Fuchsia hanging basket

Fuchsia, *Fuchsia* 'Mrs. Lovell Swisher'

SEASONAL HOUSE

Upper: Fuchsia and Hydrangea display
Lower: *Hydrangea* 'Ayesha'

Fuchsia, *Fuchsia* 'Roesse Blacky'

MAY

47

A

B

C

C

D

E

See page 130

48

Upper: *Hosta* 'St. Paul'
Lower: *Helleborus* 'Ivory Prince'; Variegated Boxwood, *Buxus sempervirens* 'Variegata'

ENTRY VESTIBULE

Orchid, *Laeliocattleya* hybrid

Orchid, *Coelogyne pandurata*

Upper: Yellow Lady Slipper Orchid, *Paphiopedilum* hybrid

Lower: Yellow Orchid, *Phalaenopsis* 'Dragon's Gold'

Spotted Lady Slipper Orchid, *Phragmipedium*

See page 130

52

FERN HOUSE

Peach Anthurium, *Anthurium andraeanum*

Painted Tongue, *Salpiglossis sinuata* 'Royal Mix'

JUNE

Homage in Green ceiling by Richard T. Spaulding

Clockwise from upper left: Entry ceiling and Peacock Light; Variegated Kousa Dogwood, *Cornus kousa* 'Variegata'; Exterior View; *Homage in Green* plaque

Sky Plant, *Tillandsia ionantha*

Upper: Bromeliad, *Aechmea hybrid*
Lower: Bromeliad, *Neoregelia hybrid*

See page 130

Reflection Pond

FERN HOUSE

Upper: Pale Pitcher Plant flower, *Sarracenia suffruticosa*
Lower: Pale Pitcher Plant, *Sarracenia leucophylla*

Birds Nest Fern fiddlehead, *Asplenium nidus*

JUNE

Purple Vanda Orchid, *Vanda* 'Tokyo Blue Sky'

Green & Magenta Orchid, *Phalaenopsis* hybrid

PALM HOUSE

Orchid, *Dendrobium thyrsiflorum*

Orchid, *Vanda* 'Miss Joaquim'

Purple Hollyhock, *Alcea rosea* 'Queeny Purple'

ENTRY VESTIBULE & OUTSIDE

JULY

Veined Orchid, *Doritaenopsis* 'Tai Lin Angel'

PALM HOUSE

Red & Gold Orchid, *Phalaenopsis* hybrid

See page 130

68

PALM HOUSE

Upper: *Anthurium andreanum*
Lower: Peacock Plant, *Calathea veitchiana*

Pigtail Anthurium, *Anthurium scherzerianum*

Astilbe 'Vision in Pink'

Upper: Gazing Ball with *Impatiens* 'Super Elfin Pink', Purple Hollyhocks, *Alcea rosea* 'Queeny Purple'
Lower: Lavender & Pink Delphiniums, *Delphinium* 'Astolat'

SEASONAL HOUSE

See page 130

JULY

Clockwise from upper left: Pocketbook Flower, *Calceolaria* 'Kentish Hero'; Flowering Maple, *Abutilon* 'Thomas Hobbs';
Croton, *Codiaeum* 'Variegatum'; Fern House display

FERN HOUSE

See page 131

JULY

See page 131

Upper: Cactus, *Mammillaria crinita*
Lower: Fox Tail Agave, *Agave attenuata*

CACTUS HOUSE

Cactus, *Parodia magnifica*

Bromeliad, *Aechmea chantinii*

Bromeliad, *Guzmania* hybrid

BROMELIAD HOUSE

Bromeliad display

Over 'lyre kinetic sculpture instrument by Dan Senn

Stargazer Lily, *Lilium* 'Stargazer'; Hollyhocks, *Alcea rose* 'Queeny Purple'; Coleus, *Solenostemon x* hybrid

SEASONAL HOUSE

AUGUST

Stargazer Lily, *Lilium* 'Stargazer' closeup

Clockwise from upper left: Container with Dusty Miller, *Senecio cineraria* 'Cirrus' and Ornamental Oregano, *Origanum rotundifolium* 'Kent Beauty'; Exterior of Bromeliad House; Indoor Passion Vine tendril; Tobacco Plant *Nicotiana* 'Only the Lonely', *Geranium* 'Orbit Hot Pink', *Lobelia* 'Crystal Palace Blue'

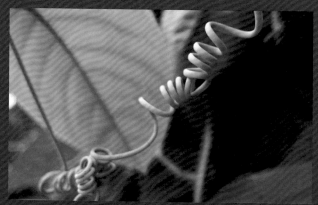

OUTSIDE

See page 131

Throatwort, *Trachelium* 'Devotion Series Purple'; *Canna* 'Red King Humbert'; Purple Fountain Grass, *Pennisetum setaceum* 'Rubrum'

ENTRY VESTIBULE

Purple Throatwort, *Trachelium* 'Devotion Series Purple'

Clockwise from upper left: Coleus, *Solenostemon* 'Glasshouse Works Trailing Plum'; *Rainforest* bell by Toshiko Takaezu; *Fuchsia triphylla* 'Gartenmeister Bonstedt'; PeeGee Hydrangea, *Hydrangea paniculata*

SEASONAL HOUSE

AUGUST

Angels Trumpets, *Brugmansia* 'Ecuador Pink'

FERN HOUSE

Upper: Yellow Angels Trumpets, *Brugmansia* hybrid
Lower: Kaffir Lily, *Clivia miniata*

Angels Trumpet, *Brugmansia* 'Ecuador Pink'

Upper: Lily of the Nile, *Agapanthus* 'Black Pantha'
Lower: Bolivian Begonia, *Begonia boliviensis* 'Bonfire'

FERN HOUSE

Tropical Rhododendron, *Vireya* 'Ne Plus Ultra'

Sensitive Plant, *Mimosa pudica*

Orange Coleus, *Solenostemon x* hybrid

SEASONAL HOUSE

SEPTEMBER

See page 132

SEASONAL HOUSE

Upper: Princess Flower, *Tibouchina urvilleana*
Lower: Korean Chrysanthemum, cultivar unknown

See page 132 **SEPTEMBER** 93

Clockwise from upper left: Fiery Costus, *Costus igneus;* Fan Palm frond, *Washingtonia filifera;* Red Lady Slipper Orchid, *Paphiopedilum hybrid;* Lacy Tree Philodendron, *Philodendron selloum*

PALM HOUSE

Shell Ginger, *Alpinia zerumbet* 'Variegata'

See page 132

CACTUS HOUSE

Succulent Rosettes, clockwise from upper left: Black Rose Aeonium, *Aeonium* 'Schwarzkopf'; White Mexican Rose, *Echeveria elegans; Echeveria* 'Perle von Nurenberg'; Variegated Pinwheel, *Aeonium haworthii* 'Variegata'

FERN HOUSE

See page 132

Upper: Flamingo Flower, *Justicia rosea*
Lower: Cape Primrose, *Streptocarpus* 'Megan'

Peace Lily, *Spathiphyllum* hybrid

SEPTEMBER

A

B

A

C

D

G

E

F

See page 133

Upper: Bromeliad, *Vriesea ospinae*
Lower: Bromeliad, *Guzmania hybrid*

BROMELIAD HOUSE

Upper: Hanging Orchid Cactus flower basket,
Epiphyllum darahii
Lower: Colorful Bromeliad, *Aechmea berteroniana*

Orchid Cactus, *Epiphyllum darahii*

Angels Trumpet, *Brugmansia* 'Ecuador Pink'

PALM HOUSE

OCTOBER

Rainforest Japanese bell by Toshiko Takaezu

SEASONAL HOUSE

Upper: PeeGee Hydrangea, *Hydrangea paniculata*
Lower: Chrysanthemum buds, *Chrysanthemum* 'Manhattan'

Sogetsu School Ikebana Chrysanthemum arrangement

Left: Chrysanthemum 'Manhattan'
Middle: Sogetsu School Ikebana Chrysanthemum arrangement
Right: Chrysanthemum 'Fall Delano'

SEASONAL HOUSE

See page 133

Christmas Pride, *Ruellia macrantha*

Upper: Carnivorous Tropical Pitcher Plant, *Nepenthes alata*

Lower: Coleus, *Solenostemon* 'Peter's Wonder'

FERN HOUSE

Peach Angels Trumpet, *Brugmansia* hybrid; *Anthurium andreanum;*
Oak-leaf Croton, *Codiaeum variegatum*

White *Cattleya* Orchid, *Miltassia*

NOVEMBER

Exhibition Style *Chrysanthemum* 'Lili Gallon'

SEASONAL HOUSE

See page 133

See page 134

Upper: *Chrysanthemum* 'Fire Island'
Lower: *Chrysanthemum* 'Kermit'

SEASONAL HOUSE

Exhibition Style *Chrysanthemum* 'Crimson Tide'   NOVEMBER   115

Clockwise from upper left: Pink & Green Sweetheart Flower, *Anthurium andraeanum;* Coral Sweetheart Flower, *Anthurium andraeanum;* Peace Lily, *Spathiphyllum* hybrid; Red & Green Sweetheart Flower, *Anthurium andraeanum*

PALM HOUSE

Cashmere Bouquet, *Clerodendrum philippinum*

See page 134

Upper: Tropical Rhododendron, *Vireya* 'Mt. Ophir'
Lower: Red & Purple Bromeliad Flower, *Aechmea sp.*

FERN & BROMELIAD HOUSE

Red Bromeliad Flower

DECEMBER

DECEMBER

Poinsettia, *Euphorbia pulcherrima* hybrid;
Peperomia obtusifolia 'Variegata';
Brazilian Candles, *Pavonia multiflora*;
Fortnight Lily, *Dietes iridioides*

Upper: Brazilian Candles, *Pavonia multiflora*
Lower: Poinsettia, actual flowers

ENTRY VESTIBULE

See page 134

Upper: Begonia, *Begonia* 'Sophie Cecile'
Lower: Cape Primrose, *Streptocarpus* 'Megan'

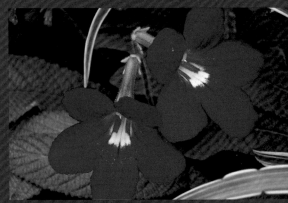

FERN HOUSE

See page 134

Silver Vase Bromeliad, *Aechmea fasciata*

Bromeliads left to right: *Guzmania* hybrid; Guzmania hybrid
Silver Vase Bromeliad, *Aechmea fasciata*

BROMELIAD HOUSE

Christmas Cactus, *Schlumbergera bridgesii*

Christmas Cactus, *Schlumbergera bridgesii*

Keys to Plant Identification

JANUARY

Page 10 (Seasonal House)

A Gardenia, *Gardenia jasminoides*
B Cast Iron Plant, *Aspidistra elatior*
C White Cyclamen, *Cyclamen persicum*
D White Evergreen Florist Azalea, *Rhododendron* hybrid
E Fortnight Lily, *Dietes iridoides*
F Pink Evergreen Florist Azalea, *Rhododendron* hybrid
G Variegated Algerian Ivy, *Hedera canariensis variegata*
H Delta Maidenhair Fern, *Adiantum raddianum*
I Pink Cineraria, *Senecio hybridus*
J Spider Plant, *Chlorophytum comosum* 'Variegatum'
K Norfolk Island Pine, *Araucaria heterophylla*

Pages 14–15 (Fern House)

A Mexican Breadfruit, *Monstera deliciosa*
B Fan Palm, species unknown
C Tiger Fern, *Nephrolepis* 'Tiger'
D Caribbean Copper Plant, *Euphorbia continifolia*
E Lady Palm, *Rhapis excelsa*
F Flaming Glorybower, *Clerodendrum speciosissimum*
G Flaming Glorybower, *Clerodendrum speciosissimum*
H Garden Croton, *Codiaeum* 'Variegatum'
I *Dracaena* 'Lemon Lime'
J Rhapis Palm or Lady Palm, *Rhapis excelsa*
K Caribbean Copper Plant, *Euphorbia continifolia*
L Red Anthurium, *Anthurium andreanum*

FEBRUARY

Page 23 (Fern House)

A Rhapis Palm or Lady Palm, *Rhapis excelsa*
B Black Ginger, *Zingiber malaysianum* 'Midnight'
C Croton, *Codiaeum variegatum*
D Red & Green Anthurium, *Anthurium andraeanum*
E Red Anthurium, *Anthurium andraeanum*
F Baby Rubber Plant, *Peperonia obtusifolia*
G Boston fern, *Nephrolepis exaltata*
H *Draceana deremensis* 'Lemon Lime'
I Reiger Begonia, *Begonia x hiemalis*
J Delta Maidenhair Fern, *Adiantum raddianum*

MARCH

Page 29 (Seasonal House)

A Easter Lily, *Lilium longiflorum* 'Nellie White'
B White Bleeding Heart, *Dicentra spectabilis alba*
C Mophead Hydrangea, *Hydrangea macrophylla*
D Cast Iron Plant, *Aspidistra elatior*
E Variegated Algerian Ivy, *Hedera canariensis variegata*
F Fortnight Lily, *Dietes iridioides*
G Delta Maidenhair Fern, *Adiantum raddianum*
H Variegated Tulips
I Pink Bleeding Heart, *Dicentra spectabilis*
J Outside, Cherry Tree

Keys to Plant Identification

Page 30 (Cactus House)

A *Cereus forbesii*
B *Mammillaria carnea*
C Tom Thumb Cactus, *Parodia mammulosa*
D Cardon Grande, *Echinopsis terscheckii*
E Cardon Grande, *Echinopsis terscheckii*
F *Mammillaria dixanthocentron*
G Silken Pincushion, *Mammillaria bombycina*
H *Mammillaria crinita*
I Golden Ball Cactus, *Parodia leninghausii*
J Peruvian Old Man Cactus, *Espostoa lanata*
K Silver Ball Cactus, *Parodia scopa*
L Wooly Torch, *Pilosocereus leucocephala*
M *Mammillaria carmenae*
N *Thelocactus rinconensis*
O Bishop's Cap Cactus, *Astrophytum myriostigma*
P Monk's Hood Cactus, *Astrophytum ornatum*
Q *Austrocephalocereus sp.*
R *Mammillaria rhodantha ssp. fera-rubra*
S Twin-spined Cactus, *Mammillaria geminispina*
T Birdsnest Cactus, *Mammillaria camptotricha*
U Snowball Cactus, *Mammillaria bocasana*
V Mexican Fence Post Cactus, *Pachycereus marginatus*

Page 33 (Fern House)

A Reiger Begonia, *Begonia x hiemalis*
B Burgundy Coleus, *Solenostemon* 'Scarlet Poncho'
C *Chirita flavimaculata*
D Blue Mist Flower, *Eupatorium atrorubens*
E Delta Maidenhair Fern, *Adiantum raddianum*
F Cape Primrose, *Streptocarpus* 'Megan'
G Spider Plant, *Chlorophytum comosum* 'Variegatum'
H Chenille Plant, *Acalypha hispida*
I Birds Nest Fern, *Asplenium nidus*

APRIL

Page 36 (Seasonal House)

A Gardenia Tree, *Gardenia jasminoides*
B Cast Iron Plant, *Aspidistra elatior*
C Delta Maidenhair Fern, *Adiantum raddianum*
D Easter Lily, *Lilium longiflorum* 'Nellie White'
E Blue Cineraria, *Senecio cruentus*
F Baby Rubber Plant, *Peperomia obtusifolia*
G White Cyclamen, *Cyclamen persicum*
H White Mophead Hydrangea, *Hydrangea macrophylla*
I Pink Evergreen Florist Azalea, *Rhododendron* hybrid

Page 42 (Cactus House)

A Twin-spined Cactus, *Mammillaria geminispina*
B *Mammillaria elongata* 'Irish Red'
C Century Plant, *Agave americana*
D Blue Candle Cactus, *Myrtillocactus geometrizans*
E Desert Rose, *Adenium obesum*
F Madagascar Palm, *Pachypodium lamerei*

Keys to Plant Identification

G Indian Spurge Tree, *Euphorbia neriifolia*
H Silver Torch Cactus, *Cleistocactus strausii*
I *Ferocactus chrysacanthus*
J Golden Barrel Cactus, *Echinocactus grusonii*
K Saguaro Cactus, *Carnegiea gigantea*

MAY

Page 48 (Entry Vestibule)
A New Zealand Flax, *Phormium* 'Maori Queen'
B *Fatsia japonica* 'Spider's Web'
C *Hosta* 'St. Paul'
D Variegated Algerian Ivy, *Hedera canariensis variegata*
E Golden Sedge Grass, *Hakonechloa macra* 'Aureola'

Page 52 (Fern House)
A Reiger Begonia, *Begonia x hiemalis*
B Chenille Plant, *Acalypha hispida*
C Beefsteak Begonia, *Begonia x erythrophylla*
D Purple False Eranthemum, *Pseuderanthemum atropupureum*
E Magenta Orchid Cactus, *Epicactus* hybrid
F Split-leaf Philodendron, *Monstera deliciosa*
G Cape Primrose, *Streptocarpus* 'Megan'
H Delta Maidenhair Fern, *Adiantum raddianum*
I Reiger Begonia, *Begonia x hiemalis*
J Spider Plant, *Chlorophytum comosum variegatum*
K Coleus, *Solenostemon* 'Scarlet Poncho'

JUNE

Page 59 (Bromeliad House)
A *Tillandsia* 'Victoria'
B Shirley Temple Plant, *Tillandsia streptophylla*
C *Tillandsia sp.*
D Spanish Moss, *Tillandsia usneoides*
E *Tillandsia schiedeana* 'Minor'
F Bromeliad *Achmea* 'Seneca'
G *Tillandsia recurvifolia ssp. subsecundifolia*

JULY

Page 68 (Palm House)
A Tropical Pitcher Plant, *Nephenthes sp.*
B Pigtail Anthurium, *Anthurium scherzerianum*
C Croton, *Codiaeum* 'Variegatum'
D Japanese Mondo Grass, *Ophiopogon jaburan* 'Variegata'
E Lacy Tree Philodendron, *Philodendron selloum*
F Anthurium, *Anthurium oblanceolata*
G Tricolor Stromanthe, *Stromanthe sanguinea* 'Tricolor'
H Carribean Copper Plant, *Euphorbia cotinifolia*
I Variegated Shell Ginger, *Alpinia zerumbet variegata*

Page 71 (Seasonal House)
A Delphinium, *Delphinium* 'Astolat'
B Canna Lily, *Canna* 'Red King Humbert'
C Coleus, *Solenostemon* 'Wizard Velvet Red'

D Tricolor Coleus, *Solenostemon x* hybrid
E False Spirea, *Astilbe* 'Vision Purple'
F Coleus, *Solenostemon* 'Sunlover Rustic Orange'
G Delta Maidenhair Fern, *Adiantum raddianum*
H Spider Plant, *Chlorophytum comosum* 'Variegatum'
I Sweet Potato Vine, *Ipomea batatas* 'Marguerite'
J Fortnight Lily, *Dietes iridioides*
K Pink False Spirea, *Astilbe* 'Vision in Pink'
L Purple Hollyhock, *Alcea rosea* 'Queeny Purple'
M Coleus, *Solenostemon* 'Glasshouse Works Trailing Plum'

Page 73 (Fern House)

A Sago Palm, *Cycas revoluta*
B Prayer Plant, *Calathea orbiculata*
C Sago Palm, *Cycas revoluta*
D Japanese Holly Fern, *Cyrtomium falcatum*
E Yellow Reiger Begonia, *Begonia x hiemalis*
F *Philodendron* 'Imperial Red'
G Sweet Potato Vine, *Ipomea batatas* 'Marguerite'
H Tiger Fern, *Nephrolepis exaltata* 'Tiger'
I Pocketbook Flower, *Calceolaria* 'Kentish Hero'
J Elephant Ear, *Alocasia odora*
K Delta Maidenhair Fern, *Adiantum raddianum*
L Birds Nest Fern, *Asplenium nidus* 'Victoria'
M Deers Tongue Fern, *Asplenium scolopendrium*
N Rose Painted Calathea, *Calathea roseopicta*
O Giant Birds Nest Fern, *Asplenium nidus*
P Robust Australian Tree Fern, *Cyathea cooperi* 'Brentwood'

Q Cardboard Palm, *Zamia furfuracea*
R Foxtail Fern, *Asparagus densiflorus* 'Myers'
S Crocodile Fern, *Microsorum musifolium*

Page 74 (Cactus House)

A Madagascar Palm, *Pachypodium lamerei*
B Blue Candle Cactus, *Myrtillocactus geometrizans*
C Desert Rose, *Adenium obesum*
D *Notocactus magnifica*
E Black Rose Aeonium, *Aeonium* 'Schwarzkopf'
F Golden Barrel Cactus, *Echinocactus grusonii*
G Century Plant, *Agave americana*

AUGUST

Page 81 (Exterior flower bed)

A Tobacco Plant, *Nicotiana* 'Only the Lonely'
B Bears Breech, *Acanthus mollis*
C Tobacco Plant, *Nicotiana* 'Perfume Deep Purple'
D Petunia, *Petunia* 'Ultra Blue Star'
E Dusty Miller, *Senecio cineraria* 'Cirrus'
F *Geranium* 'Tango Violet'
G *Lobelia* 'Crystal Palace Blue'
H Diablo Ninebark, *Physocarpus* 'Diablo'
I Strawberry Tree, *Arbutus unedo*
J Purple Heliotrope, *Heliotrope* 'Marine'

Page 85 (Seasonal House)

A Purple Throatwort, *Trachelium* 'Devotion in Purple'

B Coleus, *Solenostemon* 'Wizard Velvet Red'
C Throatwort, *Trachelium* 'Devotion in Burgundy'
D Coleus, *Solenostemon* 'Sunlover Rustic Orange'
E Red & Yellow Coleus, *Solenostemon x hybrid*
F Canna Lily, *Canna* 'Red King Humbert'
G Fortnight Lily, *Dietes iridioides*
H Sweet Potato Vine, *Ipomea batatas* 'Marguerite'
I Coleus, *Solenostemon* 'Glasshouse Works Trailing Plum'
J Delta Maidenhair Fern, *Adiantum raddianum*

SEPTEMBER

Page 92 (Seasonal House)
A Mother-in-Laws Tongue, *Sansevieria* 'Black Coral'
B Heuchera, *Heuchera* 'Lime Rickey'
C Deers Tongue Fern, *Asplenium scolopendrium*
D Deers Tongue Fern, *Asplenium scolopendrium*
E Chrysanthemum, *Chrysanthemum* 'Apricot Blush'
F Cape Fuchsia, *Phygelius* 'Lemon Frost'
G Feather Reed Grass, *Calamagrostis* 'Karl Foerster'

Page 93 (Seasonal House)
A PeeGee Hydrangea, *Hydrangea paniculata*
B Delta Maidenhair Fern, *Adiantum raddianum*
C Burgundy Coleus, *Solenostemon x* hybrid
D Korean Chrysanthemum
E Sweet Potato Vine, *Ipomea batatas* 'Marguerite'
F Purple Fountain Grass, *Pennisetum setaceum* 'Atropurpurea'

Page 96 (Cactus House)
A Cactus *Parodia magnifica*
B Compass Barrel Cactus, *Ferocactus cylindraceus*
C Red Torch Cactus, *Echinopsis huascha*
D Silver Torch Cactus, *Cleistocactus strausii*
E Old Man of the Andes, *Oreocereus celsianus*
F Mexican Grass Tree, *Dasylirion longissimum*
G Squid Agave, *Agave bracteosa*
H Variegated Agave
I Saguaro cactus, *Carnegiea gigantea*
J Gold Spine Barrel Cactus, *Ferocactus chrysacanthus*
K Saguaro cactus, *Carnegiea gigantea*
L Madagascar Palm, *Pachypodium lamerei*
M *Aloe vera*
N *Cereus argentinensis*
O Artichoke Agave, *Agave parryi v. truncata*
P Blue Candle Cactus, *Myrtillocactus geometrizans*
Q Monstrose Night Blooming Cereus, *Cereus hildmannianus* 'Monstrose'
R Foxtail agave, *Agave attenuata*
S Indian Spurge Tree, *Euphorbia neriifolia*

Page 98 (Fern House)
A Variegated False Eranthemum, *Pseuderanthemum carruthersii* 'Variegatum'
B Cape Primrose, *Streptocarpus* 'Megan'
C Peace Lily, *Spathiphyllum hybrid*

D Chenille Plant, *Acalypha hispida*
E Coleus, *Solenostemon x* hybrid
F Tiger Fern, *Nephrolepis* 'Tiger'
G Flamingo Flower, *Justicia rosea*
H False Eranthemum, *Pseuderanthemum atropupureum*
I Variegated False Eranthemum, *Pseuderanthemum carruthersii* 'Variegatum'
J Spider Plant, *Chlorophtum comosum* 'Variegatum'
K Delta Maidenhair Fern, *Adiantum raddianum*

Page 100 (Bromeliad House)

A Spanish Moss, *Tillandsia usneoides*
B *Tillandsia sp.*
C *Tillandsia leonamiana*
D *Pepinia sanguinea x Pitcairnea pseudoundulata*
E Delta Maidenhair Fern, *Adiantum raddianum*
F Bromeliad, *Guzmania* hybrid
G Sago Palm, *Cycas revoluta*

OCTOBER

Page 107 (Seasonal House)

A Pink Impatiens, *Impatiens* 'Super Elfin Pink'
B Purple Fountain Grass, *Pennisetum setaceum* 'Atropurpurea'
C Burgundy Coleus, *Solenostemon x* hybrid
D Chrysanthemum, *Chrysanthemum* 'Fall Delano'
E Delta Maidenhair Fern, *Adiantum raddianum*

NOVEMBER

Pages 112–113 (Seasonal House)

A Princess flower, *Tibuchina urvilleana*
B Green Pompom Chrysanthemums, *Chrysanthemum* 'Kermit'
C Red & Yellow Coleus, *Solenostemon x* hybrid
D Coleus, *Solenostemon* 'Stained Glassworks Trailing Plum'
E Pheasant's Tail Grass, *Stipa arundinacea*
F Sweet Potato Vine, *Ipomea batatas* 'Marguerite'
G Delta Maidenhair Fern, *Adiantum raddianum*
H Purple Fountain Grass, *Pennisetum setaceum* 'Atropurpurea'
I Burgundy Coleus large leaf, *Solenostemon x* hybrid
J Rabbits Foot Fern, *Polypodium aureum*
K Cascade Chrysanthemum, *Chrysanthemum* 'Bronze Fleece'
L Coleus, *Solenostemon* 'Sunlover Rustic Orange'
M Fortnight Lily, *Dietes iridioides*
N Canna Lily, *Canna* 'Red King Humbert'
O New Zealand Flax, *Phormium* 'Shirazz'
P Giant Yucca, *Yucca elephantipes*
Q Pheasant's Tail Grass, *Stipa arundinacea*
R Exhibition Style Chrysanthemum, *Chrysanthemum* 'Bola De Oro'
S Chrysanthemum, *Crysanthemum* 'Fall Delano'
T Zebra Grass, *Miscanthus sinensis* 'Zebrinus'
U Cast Iron Plant, *Aspidistra elatior*

Keys to Plant Identification

Page 114 (Seasonal House)

A Chinese Exhibition Chrysanthemum, *Chrysanthemum* 'Ni Jin Biao' (translation: Golden and dull brown striped leopard)
B Coleus, *Solenostemon* 'Stained Glasshouse Trailing Plum'
C Delta Maidenhair Fern, *Adiantum raddianum*
D Chrysanthemum, *Chrysanthemum* 'Fire Island'
E Red & Yellow Coleus, *Solenostemon x* hybrid
F Sweet Potato Vine, *Ipomea batatas* 'Marguerite'
G Cascade Chrysanthemum, *Chrysanthemum* 'Bronze Fleece'
H Delta Maidenhair Fern, *Adiantum raddianum*
I Purple Fountain Grass, *Pennisetum setaceum* 'Atropurpurea'
J Ficus, *Ficus* 'Midnight'

Page 118 (Fern House)

A Lady Palm, *Rhapis excelsa*
B Croton, *Codiaeum variegatum pictum*
C Philodendron 'Lemon Lime'
D Tiger Fern, *Nephrolepis exaltata* 'Tiger'
E Thanksgiving Cactus, *Schlumbergera truncata*
F Sensitive Plant, *Mimosa pudica*
G Sweet Potato Vine, *Ipomea batatas* 'Marguerite'
H Sweetheart Flower, *Anthurium andreanum*

DECEMBER

Page 123 (Seasonal House)

A Red Poinsettia
B *Peperomia obtusifolia* 'Variegata'

C Variegated Algerian Ivy, *Hedera canariensis variegata*
D Delta Maidenhair Fern, *Adiantum raddianum*
E Cast Iron Plant, *Aspidistra elatior*
F *Hebe* 'Quicksilver'
G Fortnight Lily, *Dietes iridioides*
H Sweet Olive, *Osmanthus fragrans*
I *Pittosporum tenuifolium*
J New Zealand Flax, *Phormium* 'Shirazz'
K Christmas Tree
L White Poinsettia, *Euphorbia pulcherrima* 'White Star'

Page 125 (Fern House)

A Begonia 'Sophie Cecile'
B Coleus, *Solenostemon* 'Peter's Wonder'
C Rita's Gold Fern, *Nephrolepis* 'Rita's Gold'
D Pseuderanthemum carruthersii 'Variegatum'
E Corpse Plant in leaf stage, *Amorphophallus titanum*
F *Anthurium* 'Congo Green'
G Trailing Variegated Ivy, *Hedera helix* 'Glacier'
H Spider plant, *Clorophytum comosum* 'Variegata'
I Delta Maidenhair Fern, *Adiantum raddianum*
J Cape Primrose, *Streptocarpus* 'Megan'
K Multicolor Coleus, *Solenostemon x* hybrid
L Mother Fern, *Asplenium bulbiferum*
M Peace Lily, *Spathiphyllum* hybrid
N Bromeliad, *Billbergia* hybrid

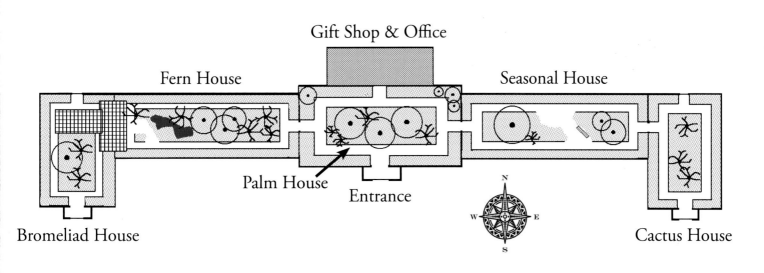

Gift Shop & Office

Fern House

Seasonal House

Palm House

Bromeliad House

Entrance

Cactus House

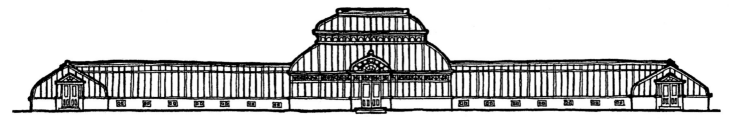

Index

Index

Index

Prize-winning photographer, blue-ribbon gardener (and daughter of a Master Gardener and avid photographer), Sara L. Chapman has gardened and photographed in New York, Florida, California and Washington State. She has taken photos around the world, with a life-long interest in scenic, flower and garden photography. Sara received her first camera, a Kodak Brownie, as a child, and studied photography at the School of Visual Arts in New York City.

Sara is a graphic artist and designer, since 1999 owning Art Squad Graphics, a graphic arts studio that specializes in book design. She also owns lovethatimage.com, a photography website. Sara is active in the national Graphic Artists Guild and currently serves as President of the Seattle chapter.

Like Monet, she gardens to have good photo subjects. She now gardens and photographs in Seattle, Washington.

Free download at lovethatimage.com:

"7 Secrets to Better Flower Photography—
Simple and Easy!"